Hoot Owl Hollow

By

Jill Glassco

Illustrated by Ben Glassco

Deep Sea Publishing, LLC

Copyright Page

ISBN-13: 978-1-939535-60-3
ISBN: 1939535603

www.deepseapublishing.com

Printed in the United States of America

Table of Contents

Dedicated to my brother,

Dr. Mark Watson,

who has faithfully served pets and their families in the

Cumberland Gap of Kentucky

for over 30 years.

A kinder and gentler man you will never meet.

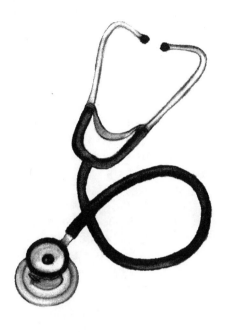

Chapter 1:
The Great Escape

ndi took another bite of the smoked turkey sandwich. *If the ad's still there, I'm applying tonight*, she thought. Checking over her shoulder to make sure no one was watching, the attractive, young woman snatched the Atlanta News from the break room table and scanned the classified section. "Here it is," she said.

WANTED: Male DVM willing to work in rugged conditions.

Apply to: Dr. Sam Parks, 202 Buckeye Rd., Bottle Knob, GA 30546

She jotted the name and address on a notepad and buried it in her coat pocket.

After graduation, Dr. Andrea Ruth Elliott had leaped at the opportunity to work at a thriving veterinary clinic in Atlanta, Georgia. Within a few short weeks of taking the position, however, the country girl from North Carolina questioned her hasty decision. Living in a skyscraper-and-concrete world made her feel like a right hand jammed into a left-handed glove.

That evening, she placed the note beside her computer and typed:

> **Dear Dr. Parks,**
>
> **My name is Andy Elliott, and I am writing in regards to your ad in the Atlanta News. In May, I graduated with honors from the College of Veterinary Medicine at Auburn University and am currently employed at a prestigious small animal clinic in Atlanta.**
>
> **I am very interested in the DVM position at Bottle Knob and consider the rugged conditions to be a welcomed challenge, not a deterrent. I would greatly appreciate the opportunity to interview for this position and look forward to hearing from you soon.**
>
> **Sincerely,**
>
> *Andy*
>
> **Dr. A. R. Elliott**

With crossed fingers, she folded the letter and slid it into an envelope. *I'm not really being dishonest*, the girl convinced herself. *After all, "Andi" is just a nickname, and I can spell it anyway I want to, can't I? Hopefully, this backwoods Dr. Parks won't have a computer or even know how to look up my name.*

Two weeks later, Andi pulled her sunshine-yellow beetle alongside the wall of apartment postboxes. A quick thumb through the mail uncovered her hopes near the bottom of the stack — a hand-addressed letter to "Dr. Andy Elliott":

> Andy,
>
> I'm up to my eyeballs in cows, horses, goats, and pigs — let alone dogs and cats. Don't have time for interviews. Just be forewarned that I'm the only vet in the county, the work's hard, the hours are long, and the pay's low, but if you still want the job, it's yours. Let me know if you're coming, and try to get here by the end of next week.
>
> Sam

"Yes!" Andi said. "Now, if I can just convince this man to let me stay once he learns that Dr. Andy Elliott is female."

2

The next morning, she sent a reply saying she would arrive the following week and then gave Dr. Rainwater her resignation along with an apology for such short notice.

On her last day at the Magnolia Springs Animal Clinic, Jack, the vet tech, said, "I can't believe you're doing this, Andi. Givin' up a good paying job with one of the best veterinarians in Georgia to move to who knows where, to work for who knows who, and to do who knows what. It's like stepping backwards forty years. And what if this Dr. Parks won't even let you stay when he finds out you're a girl? What are you thinkin'?"

She stuffed her stethoscope into the medical bag and snapped it closed. "I'm thinkin' that I can't get out of this city and up to those mountains fast enough. Look, Jack, I appreciate your concern, but my mind's made up. And besides, Dr. Rainwater was kind enough to invite me back if things don't work out."

"Well, please be careful," Jack said. "And I hope you find whatever it is you're looking for."

She gave her friend a hug. "Thanks, Jack," she said and then walked out the door.

Andi crawled along the congested freeway until she reached the edge of the mountains north of Atlanta. Under the clear, summer sky, she stopped on the shoulder of the highway to lower the convertible top and studied the smoky-gray foothills of the Blue Ridge Mountain chain holding Grandfather Mountain – the highest peak near her grandparents' farm. She took a deep breath and said, "I'm free!"

With the breeze in her face and a fresh wind in her spirit, the determined doctor maneuvered the snaking road through the Chattahoochee National Forest. She understood why the Cherokee Native Americans had named these beautiful woodlands "Sah-ka-ná-ga" meaning "The Great Blue Hills of God".

Two hours later, she saw Chatuge Lake sparkling in the distance and the road marker: "Bottle Knob, 3 miles ahead." Her cloud-nine excitement melted into a puddle of apprehension. *Oh, mercy. What have I gotten myself into?* she thought.

Bottle Knob reminded her of home. Gaslights on green poles lined Main Street — a checkerboard thoroughfare of neighborhood stores. Toward the center of the quaint town, she found the local post office. Wrought iron rails framed the concrete steps on this traditional red brick building constructed in the 1930s, and an ornate cupola and weathervane topped the rusty tin roof.

3

Inside, Andi approached a middle-aged man behind the mail counter. "Hello. I'm Andi Elliott. Could you tell me how to find the veterinary clinic on Buckeye Road, please?"

"Andy, did you say? You lookin' for Doc Sam?" he said. The man's eyebrows lifted behind his spectacles, and his mouth twitched to a half grin.

"Yes, sir."

"Well now, jest head on out of town by way of Main Street and take the first right – that's Buckeye Road. The clinic's 'bout a quarter mile down that road on yer left. You can't miss it, little lady. Doc's expectin' you."

"Thank you, sir," Andi said.

She turned to leave and heard the man chuckle. "But you're a far cry from what he's expectin'," he mumbled.

Within minutes, Andi located the rustic log cabin with a hand-painted "Bottle Knob Animal Clinic" sign hanging on the front porch and pulled her beetle onto the gravel lot. Dogs in the backyard kennels barked when she opened the car door.

She made her way up the stone steps and between the cane-bottomed rockers sitting on the porch. The summa cum laude DVM felt like a kindergartner on the first day of school; and with a shaky hand, she reached for the brass doorknob. "Here goes," she whispered.

Reflections #1

POINTS to Ponder

1. What hasty decision did Andi regret? _____
   _____

2. What decision(s) have you made that you regret? _____
   _____

   Does God give second chances?   YES   NO   (Read the book of Jonah to discover God's second chances for Jonah and the Ninevites.)

3. Name 3 things that will help you make wise decisions. (Look for answers

   in the scriptures below.) _____

   _____

PEARLS from God's heart to yours

_____ (your name), trust in Me with all your heart and don't depend on your own understanding. In all ways, acknowledge Me, and I will direct your path. (Prov. 3:5-6)

_____ (your name), My word is a lamp unto your feet and a light unto your path. (Psalm 119:105)

_____ (your name), without consultation, plans are frustrated, but with many [godly] counselors they succeed. (Prov. 15:22)

PETITIONS from your heart to Jesus

_____

_____

_____

_____

Chapter 2:
Hoot Owl Hollow

The simply furnished but well-kept waiting room smelled of disinfectant. A pleasant looking woman seated behind a wooden desk welcomed her with a friendly smile and said, "Hello, miss. I'm Katie Jenkins. May I help you?"

"Yes, please. I'm Andi Elliott, and I'm here to see Dr. Parks."

"So, *you're* Dr. Elliott. Welcome to Bottle Knob. I'll tell Doc Sam you're here," she said.

Katie stuck her head through the doorway behind the desk and announced, "Dr. Elliott's here to see you, Dr. Parks."

When Dr. Park's 6'4", athletic frame filled the threshold, he towered over the 5'3" lady veterinarian. The doctors stared at one another in stunned silence. The former linebacker for the University of Tennessee was anything but little or old like Andi had envisioned.

Katie's voice broke the awkward silence. "Uh, Dr. Parks, I'd like for you to meet Dr. Elliott. Dr. Elliott, this is Sam Parks."

"It's very nice to meet you Dr. Pa-" Andi started but was cut short by Sam's outburst.

"Wait a minute. My ad clearly stated that I'm looking for a male vet! I'm sorry, ma'am, but you're badly mistaken if you think I'm gonna let a woman come work for me in these mountains. You're liable to get yourself killed. "

Before Andi could retort, the front door swung open, and a boy around twelve years of age rushed in cradling a bloody Walker hound in his arms. Tears streaked his freckled cheeks and panic marked his eyes.

"I need help, Dr. Parks! Ol' Frankie's been shot. Please, kin you save him?" he sputtered.

"Bring Frankie back here, Jody, and put him on the table," Sam said.

"I'll help," Andi said and then ran to her car to retrieve her medical bag.

Katie comforted Jody in the waiting room while Sam and Andi worked side by side to save the hound. "He's more than a pet," Sam said. "Like most folks 'round these parts, Jody's family depends on this huntin' dog to help put food on the table."

An hour later, Sam came to the boy and said, "Frankie's a tough one, Jody. We got the bullet out, and he made it through the surgery just fine."

"Oh, thank you!" Jody said. "Thank ya so much, doctor."

"But he's gonna need some time to heal up and get his strength back. So go on home now and tell your mama I'll keep him here for a few days where I can keep an eye on him."

Andi was standing at the sink washing her hands when Sam returned. "You're a good surgeon, Dr. Elliott, and I could sure use your skills around here," he said. "So, I've changed my mind and decided to give you a try — one week at a time. But the first second you slow me down or even come close to gettin' yourself hurt, you're done. Is that understood?"

"Yes, Dr. Parks, I understand," Andi said. "Thank you."

"I guess you'll need a place to stay. Nonie Baskin back in Hoot Owl Hollow has a trailer out in her cow pasture that she'll rent."

Mrs. Jenkins' wrote down the directions to Nonie Baskin's farm and handed them to the tired, young woman.

"Be back here by 6:30 in the morning," Sam said.

"I will," Andi said. "And thanks again for givin' me a chance."

The last sliver of the crimson sun had dropped behind Brass Town Bald by the time Andi turned off the black top onto Hoot Owl Hollow Road. The dirt pathway wound between two tall peaks, and on the other side of the gap, a lovely cove lay hidden from the world by a wall of mountains.

Cattle grazed in the green pasture bounded by a barbed-wire fence, and toward the end of the cove, a small house and barn burrowed against the foot of the steep hills. A vintage John Deer tractor sat in the shed next to the barn, and a chicken coop and smoke house stood beyond the toolshed. A gurgling creek spilled off the mountainside and ran beside the house, into a field, and then disappeared behind the camper trailer sitting right in the middle of the cow pasture – just like Sam said.

Andi parked beside a 1978 white Chevy pickup and got out of her car. In the garden, a lone figure clad in boots and overalls hoed a row of butterbeans in the twilight. When she saw Andi, the woman picked up the bucket of fresh picked beans, threw the hoe over one shoulder, and moseyed out of the vegetable garden toward the girl.

Andi said, "Mrs. Baskin? I'm Andi Elliott. Dr. Parks said you have a trailer I can rent?"

She set the bucket and hoe at her feet, and then used her bonnet to mop the sweat from her face. "Ever'body calls me Nonie," she said.

The woman wiped one hand on a pants' leg and extended it toward the girl. "I reckin yo're that young *feller* from the city that come to work for Sam. I 'spect he wuz fit to be tied when a purdy, little gal come waltzin' through the door. I'd give my eyeteeth to uv seen his face! Well, take yer thangs on out to the camper, and I'll come out in a spell to see that ya got settled in okay. Don't forgit to latch the gate, and see to it that ya don't cut yer foot."

"Yes, ma'am. Is there broken glass in the pasture?" Andi said.

Nonie slapped her leg and cackled. "No, child. I'm meanin' don't step them fancy sandals of yorn smack-dab in the center of a cow patty."

The old woman sauntered on toward her house, shaking her head and muttering, "City folks."

Andi unloaded the car and trudged toward her new home. Thankfully, she'd packed a flashlight that helped her pick a path through the cow patties to the small trailer. She walked up the concrete block steps and opened the rusted door on the screened porch. A handmade picnic table sat on the plank floor and a close line clipped with pins stretched across the far end. She flipped the switch by the doorpost, and the yellow light bulb dangling from the ceiling by a single wire lit up like a firefly. "Hurray! I have electricity," Andi said.

The inside of the camper appeared cozy with a plaid couch on the right side of the little room and a kitchenette on the left. A red-checkered tablecloth covered a rectangle table sitting between two benches, and matching curtains framed the windows over the sink and the sofa. A two-eyed stove with a narrow oven sat beside the sink, and a refrigerator stood adjacent to the stove.

She opened the windows for fresh air, and then peeked through a curtained doorway. A simple chest of drawers and standard bed covered by a yellow, cotton-chenille spread furnished the second room. In one corner, a metal partition concealed a small shower stall, toilet, and lavatory.

At that moment, Nonie booted the trailer door making Andi jump. "It's me, gal. Come open this here door!" she hollered.

Andi hurried to the door, and Nonie stepped inside holding a heavy pot in one hand and a covered plate in the other. "Since ya got here at plumb near dark, I suspicioned ya might be hungry. Mind if I join ya for a bite of soup and cornbread?" Nonie said.

Andi welcomed the company and grabbed two spoons from a drawer and blue willow bowls from the cupboard. "That'd be great! Thank you, Miss Nonie," she said.

The old woman set the pot on the stove, dipped hot, vegetable soup into the bowls, and then joined Andi at the table. Before taking a bite, she closed her eyes and prayed, "Thank Ya, Lord Jesus, for seein' us through another day and for providin' another meal. I'm obliged to Ya, Lord, for sendin' some company to Hoot Owl Holler. And Lord, Andi's gonna need Yer help to do this hard work You've set before her, and Sam's gonna need patience – lots of patience. But I reckin You know that, Lord. Amen."

Reflections #2

POINTS to Ponder

1. Webster's dictionary defines "adventure" as an undertaking involving danger and unknown risks. Would you agree that Andi is on an adventure?

YES   NO

2. What have you done that involved unknown risks? _____

_____

3. Who or what do you depend on when you have something hard to do? _____

_____

PEARLS *from God's heart to yours*

_____ (your name), call to Me, and I will answer you, and I will tell you great and mighty things, which you do not know. (Jer. 33:3)

_____ (your name), you can do all things through Me who gives you strength. (Phil. 4:13)

_____ (your name), who will separate you from My love? Will tribulation or distress…or peril…but in all these things you overwhelmingly conquer through Me who loves you… [and nothing will be able to] separate you from the love of God, which is in Christ Jesus your Lord. (Rom. 8:35,37,39)

PETITIONS *from your heart to Jesus*

_____

_____

_____

_____

_____

Chapter 3:
Nonie Baskin

The mountain woman intrigued Andi. She learned that Nonie's only child had died at birth and that Mr. Baskin had passed away a good many years before leaving the old woman to work the farm single-handedly.

"Life ain't no fairytale, that's fer shore," Nonie said. "Why, on my own weddin' day, I worked my paw's cornfields and baked him a cake, and then that same afternoon, I married Ernest Baskin. The very next mornin', I went to work

11

on my husband's farm – a cookin' and a cleanin' fer him. Now, I jest do what I kin; and when I cain't, I swoller my stubborn pride and ask fer help. But it's mighty peaceful back here in this ol' holler. I got food on the table and a solid roof over my head. The Lord's been good to me."

"Miss Nonie, may I tell you somethin'?" Andi said. "I don't know what I've gotten myself into. I thought I was doin' the right thing comin' back to the mountains and workin' in Bottle Knob, but now I'm not so sure. I don't think I'll ever live up to Dr. Park's expectations. I made a mistake goin' to Atlanta, and now I'm afraid I've messed up again. I wish I had your strength. You live way back here all alone and run a whole farm by yourself. And you don't seem to be afraid of anything. What's your secret?"

Nonie laughed and said, "Well, first of all, it ain't my strength, child; it's the Lord's strength in me. And second of all, 'tis the set of the sails, and not the gales, that tell us the way to go'."

"That's beautiful. Did you make that up?"

Nonie grinned. "Naw. Ella Wheeler Wilcox, an American author and poet, wrote them purdy words. Life comes in seasons, Andi, and some seasons are awful hard. Ain't nothing' you kin do 'bout that, but yer attitude in the midst of the pain is yer choice. The secret is to stay saddled up close to Jesus ever'day. Talk to Him and listen to what He's got to say by stayin' under His word and goin' to His church. Then, even when ya got troubles; them troubles ain't got you. Have ya ever heared of a feller named Jehoshaphat?"

Andi shook her head and said, "No, ma'am."

"Well, ya see, way back yonder, long time ago, thar wuz this here king of Judah named Jehoshaphat. One day he got some turrible news — not one, not two, but three fearsome armies wuz a comin' against him. Well, that King Jehoshaphat, he commenced to shakin' in his boots and wuz scareder than a long-tailed cat in a rocking chair factory, so he turned his attention to seek the Lord. Oh, how that king prayed, and he called all the menfolk, women, and young'uns throughout the whole land to pray too. He howled like a coyot' bayin' at the moon. 'O God, ain't You the God of heaven? Ain't You the One that done drove out our enemies before? O God, won't You help us agin? Fer we're plumb powerless against this swarm of varmints a comin' to git us, and we don't know what to do. But Lord, we're a keepin' our eyes on You.' And ya know what the Lord did?"

Wide-eyed, Andi said, "What?"

"Well, in those days, God talked to His kids through prophets. So the Lord told one of them prophets named Jahaziel, 'You go tell ole Jehoshaphat not to be a fearin', 'cause the battle ain't his; it's Mine. Tell him to go on out thar tomorrow and jest watch Me whup them rebel rousers.'"

"What happened?" Andi said.

"Well, the very next day, Jehoshaphat wuz a trustin' the Lord somethin' fierce, so he sent the music folks out in front of his fightin' men. And whilst that choir wuz a singin' praises to God, the Lord stirred thangs up between them three legions, and they commenced to a fightin' each other. After the dust settled, not one of them rascals wuz left a standin'. So Jehoshaphat jest marched his folks right onto the battleground as purdy as you please and gathered up all the spoils. Andi, God ain't changed. He'll fight yer battles, too, when you trust Him and let Him do it."

"Hmmm," Andi said, "I never thought about it that way."

Nonie helped Andi clean the dishes then gathered her things to leave. At the door, she patted Andi's shoulder and said, "Keep that purdy, little chin up, sugar. Ever'thang's gonna be alright. You'll see. Thangs'll look brighter in the mornin'. They always do. G'night now."

From the pasture, Nonie called back, "Stop by my house before ya leave in the mornin'. I got a extry pair of rubber boots and overalls that might jest come in handy. Sweet dreams, honey."

A spring-water shower and her favorite pink, candy-striped pajamas soothed Andi's qualms. She slipped between the crisp sheets, and the next sound she heard was Clarence, Miss Nonie's Rhode Island Red rooster, waking the dawn. She sprang from the bed, threw on her work clothes, and dashed out of the trailer before the sun peeped over the horizon.

"I beat you, Mr. Sunshine," she said. "At least I won the first race of the day."

As promised, she went straight to Nonie's house and found her waiting in the porch swing.

"Mornin', honey. Here," Nonie said and handed her a brown paper bag and a small Bible with a worn, leather cover. "This buttermilk biscuit and smoked sausage'll stick to them skinny ribs of yorn, and a word or two from the Good Book will feed a hungry soul."

"Thanks, Nonie, but I've tried readin' the Bible a couple of times, and I don't really understand it."

"Don't worry 'bout understandin' ever'thang. Just keep readin', and before ya know it, the word'll go right past yer mind and right into yer spirit. Besides, the Bible's got some pow'rful good stories. The one I told you last night come straight from the Old Testamint — second Chronicles, chapter twenty," Nonie said.

"Yes, ma'am," Andi said and filled her arms with the Bible, breakfast, boots, and britches. "Thank you. I hope you have a good day, and I'll see you tonight. Wish me luck."

"No sech thang as luck, child. Only the good Lord's favor and amazin' grace."

Andi bent down, kissed her new friend's wrinkled cheek, and then scurried to the car. Leaving the farm, she rolled down the windows and watched the sunlight kiss the cool, morning air changing dewdrops to diamonds on spider webs crocheted through the night. Deep purple morning glories hugged the fencerow where Nonie's cows nibbled Bahia grass. One raised her black head and mooed when the Volkswagen scooted by. Andi laughed and refocused on getting to work on time.

Suddenly, someone jumped over the barbed wire fence, shot across the road ahead of her, and then disappeared into the woods. She slammed her brakes, and her heart pounded like a kettledrum. Then glancing at her watch, she stomped the gas pedal and sped out of the hollow with her long ponytail dancing in the wind. *You can do this, Andi*, she encouraged herself.

Reflections #3

POINTS to Ponder

1. How did Andi feel about her decision to come to Bottle Knob? _____

_____

2. What does "'tis the set of the sails, and not the gales, that tell us the way to go" mean to you? _____

_____

3. How does your attitude impact your circumstances? _____

_____

PEARLS from God's heart to yours

_____ (your name), learn to be content in whatever circumstances you have. (Phil. 4:11)

_____ (your name), rejoice always; pray without ceasing; in everything give thanks; for this is My will for you in Christ Jesus. (1 Thess. 5:16-18)

_____ (your name), have this attitude in yourself which was also in Christ Jesus... He humbled Himself by becoming obedient to the point of death, even death on a cross... Do all things without grumbling or complaining. (Phil. 2:5,8,14)

PETITIONS from your heart to Jesus

_____

_____

_____

_____

_____

Chapter 4:
Pig-Tales

D r. Parks was loading supplies into his truck when Andi got to the clinic. "Good mornin'," she said.

"Mornin'. Just hop in my truck when you're ready," Sam said. "We're goin' to Floyd Massey's farm to vaccinate pigs."

Andi pulled Nonie's clodhoppers and coveralls from the trunk, and said, "Sounds good to me. I'm ready."

"Well, uh, okay then. Let's go."

Sam's silence as they bumped over the potholes on Buckeye Road only multiplied the butterflies in Andi's stomach. She racked her brain for some way to start a conversation and finally said, "So how far is it to Mr. Massey's farm?"

"Oh, 'bout fifteen miles or so," Sam said.

"That's nice. I'll get to see more of the community. It sure is pretty up here."

He didn't reply; so after several quiet minutes, Andi tried again. "By the way, when I was leavin' Miss Nonie's today, someone came out of her pasture and ran into the woods. Who do you suppose it was? Do you think Miss Nonie's okay?"

Sam grinned and said, "Oh, I'm not worried about Nonie Baskin. She could lick a black bear with one hand tied behind her back. Maybe you saw Oukonunaka."

"Who?" Andi said.

"Oukonunaka, the legendary Owl Man of Hoot Owl Hollow. In the Cherokee language, Oukonunaka means White Owl. The story's told that in 1838 when the federal government forced 13,000 Cherokee Native Americans to leave North Georgia and march the Trail of Tears, a brave named Oukonunaka hid in a cave back in the mountains close to what's now Nonie's farm. He vowed never to leave those woodlands, and recently, some folks claim they've seen his ghost running through Hoot Owl Hollow."

"Well, this was no ghost," Andi said. "What I saw was real flesh and blood."

"Just tell Nonie. Maybe she knows who it was," Sam said.

He navigated twists and crooks through the steep hills until the knolls opened to a green valley dotted with farms. Samuel Forest Parks had grown up in Bottle Knob and loved the North Georgia Mountains. A month prior to his graduation from the School of Veterinary Medicine at the University of Tennessee in Knoxville, the town's long-time veterinarian "just happened" to decide it was time to retire. Because he'd spent every dime for school, Sam didn't have the down payment; but Dr. Pate said that an honest man's handshake was good enough for him.

When they reached the Massey farm, two dogs trotted toward the visitors wagging their tails. Sam stroked the older one. "Hey, girl. You teachin' this pup all your huntin' tricks?"

The puppy caught Sam's bootstraps between his teeth and shook his head side to side. "Hey there, Rip. I see you too, little man," Sam said, and then playfully flipped him over and patted his round, pink belly.

A man under a straw hat limped toward Sam and Andi. "Ain't *no* pup ever gonna be as smart as ole Sue. She's the best huntin' dog I ever seen," he said.

"Yes, sir, I reckon you're right about that," Sam said. "Mr. Massey, this is Dr. Andi Elliott. She came up from Atlanta to help at the clinic for a while."

Mr. Massey nodded. "How-do, ma'am. It's a pleasure meetin' ya."

Andi liked the way the old man's eyes laughed when he smiled. "The pleasure's all mine, Mr. Massey. You certainly have a beautiful place here," she said.

"Thank ya, ma'am. This farm's been in my family fer four generations," Mr. Massey said proudly.

"Well, we better get to work," Sam said. "How many piglets do you have this time, Floyd?"

"Oh, it's been a good season, Sam – a right good season. Petunia had nine babies and Bell eleven. Guess ya didn't see many hawgs in the city, did ya, Dr. Elliott?"

"Please, call me Andi," she said. "No, sir. Just dogs and cats mostly. But I used to help my grandparents on their farm. They had all kinds of animals. Sometimes, Granddaddy let me walk through the pens with him. He'd talk to his pigs and pet 'em to get 'em used to humans. He said a happy pig is a healthy pig."

"Sounds like yer grandpaw was a good farmer," Mr. Massey said. "I like 'er, Sam. I thank she's a keeper."

Sam smiled and said, "We'll see."

Andi volunteered to catch the babies and entered the holding pen. She felt like a little girl again and giggled as she chased a fat, little piglet with a gray spot over one eye.

"Here little piggy," Andi called. "Come on. I won't hurt you. Come to Andi. We're just gonna give you some medicine to make you big and strong like your mama."

Just when Andi thought she had the baby cornered, it squealed and darted between her boots. But with a fast hand, she grabbed the piglet by one leg and swung it into her arms. "It's okay, baby. This'll be over before you can say Jack Robinson on a pinto pony."

Mr. Massey slapped Sam's back and said, "Did ya see that, doc? I told ya she's a good 'un!"

Andi handed the first piglet to Mr. Massey and took off after another. Sam administered the shots and then placed the treated baby back with its sow in a separate pen. The doctors and farmer made a good team and finished the vaccinations before lunchtime.

"Kin you young folks stay fer lunch? The Mrs. is a cookin' up a big batch of turnip greens, black-eyed peas, and mashed tators."

"Thanks, Floyd, sounds delicious, but we better hit the road. Jake Stewart has a broodmare about to foal and asked me to stop by his place on the way back to the clinic," Sam said. "Maybe another time."

Back on Buckeye Road, Sam looked at Andi and said, "You did a good job this morning."

"Thanks. I gotta admit, I haven't chased pigs in a month of Sundays, but that was fun."

After checking the mare, they returned to the clinic where the waiting room was filled with locals and their pets.

"We can work faster if we divide the patients," Sam said. "Are you comfortable with that?"

"Of course," she said. "Thanks for trusting me with your clients."

Both veterinarians attended sick and wounded critters nonstop until after seven that evening. Unaccustomed to a thirteen-hour workday, Andi was relieved when Sam told her she could leave.

When she got to Hoot Owl Hollow, she spotted the mountain woman walking out of the trees carrying a burlap bag. "Hi, Miss Nonie," Andi called and waved. "What were you doin' in the woods?"

"Howdy, child," Nonie said. "Oh, jest tendin' to my chores. Are ya hungry? I got a pot of stew on the stove."

19

"I'm so hungry I could eat an opossum," Andi said. "Stew sounds wonderful."

Nonie laughed and said, "'Possum ain't so bad. You oughta try it sometime."

On the porch, the old woman stuffed the empty bag into a wooden bin beside the swing and said, "Scat on in the house now, and wash them dirty hands. I'll be in in a minute to git supper on the table, and you kin tell me all about yer day while we eat."

Andi went inside; but through the window, she caught Nonie nodding toward the trees. At the edge of the woods, the girl saw someone hunkered down in the tall weeds. Next, the man stood up, signaled back, and then vanished in the underbrush. *That's the stranger I saw this morning,* Andi thought.

Reflections #4

POINTS to Ponder

1. As a child, Andi learned about farm animals from her _____.

2. Who is a good teacher in your life? _____

   What's the most important thing that person has taught you? _____

   _____

3. Read Deut. 6:5-7. According to God, the most important thing parents should teach their children is_____.

PEARLS from God's heart to yours

_____ (your name), you shall love the Lord your God with all your heart, and with all your soul, and with all your mind. This is the great and foremost commandment. (Matt. 22:37-38)

_____ (your name), the second is like it, you shall love your neighbor as yourself. (Matt. 22:39)

_____ (your name), count all things to be loss in view of the surpassing value of knowing Christ Jesus the Lord. (Phil. 3:8a)

PETITIONS from your heart to Jesus

_____

_____

_____

_____

_____

Chapter 5:
The Stranger

At the supper table, Nonie set a plate of steaming white rice topped with roast beef, Irish potatoes, plump carrots, and sweet onions smothered in brown gravy in front of her famished tenant.

"Mmmmmmm, that smell's so good," Andi said. "Thank you."

The girl's animated story of chasing pigs at Floyd Massey's hog farm tickled Nonie. Andi laughed too, and said, "It was like tryin' to herd a bunch of stray cats!"

"I betcha ole Sam wuz surprised," Nonie said. "He pro'bly thought one day at the hawg farm would send you high-tailin' it back to the city for shore. I'm proud of ya, Andi. Yes siree Bob, mighty proud."

Andi smiled and said, "Thanks, Miss Nonie. Oh, and I meant to tell you. When I was leavin' the hollow this mornin', I saw a man come out of your pasture and run into the woods."

"You did, did ya."

"Yes, ma'am. Dr. Parks said folks 'round here claim they've seen Oukonunaka, the legendary Owl Man, but this was no legend. And after I came in the house, you nodded toward a man in the woods. Who was that?"

Nonie took another bite of stew. "This stew's right tasty, if I do say so myself," she said. "Andi, have ye ever heared tell of the prodigal son?"

"Uh, I think so," Andi said.

"Girl, how in heaven's name did ya manage to grow up in the South and come to know so little 'bout Jesus and the Bible?" Nonie said.

"Well, uh, my mama, uh, m... my parents that is, never took me to church much. Daddy always said churchgoers are just a bunch of hypocrites. But, I did go with my grandmamma and granddaddy from time to time."

"Honey, sounds like that ole devil snagged yer paw on one of his oldest hooks – a lurin' folks into settin' thar eyes on people 'stead of the Lord. As shore as eggs is eggs, people *will* disappoint ya, but Jesus Christ is true-blue yesterday and today and ferever. Anyways," Nonie said, "some years back thar wuz this man who had two sons. One day, his youngest boy come to his paw and said, 'I'm sick of workin' on this ole farm, Pop. Gimme my inheritance, and I'm gettin' out of this hick town.' Well, it 'bout broke the old man's heart. But he give that whippersnapper his share, and then watched that young feller shove the money and all his belongings in a sack. The boy throwed it over his shoulder and strutted off down the road like he wuz King Solomon hisself. T'weren't long a tall, though, till that foolish rascal done spent ever'thang he had. He wuz flat broke without a penny to his name."

Andi didn't understand what this tale had to do with "the price of tea in China," but she loved listening to the old woman's stories.

"Well, Mr. Know-it-all wuzn't so high and mighty then. So he went and hired hisself out to a farmer who sent him into the fields to slop hawgs. That boy wuz a starvin' plumb nigh to death and would've gladly filled his belly with the pods them pigs et. But nobody give him nothin'! So he come to his senses and skedaddled, lickity-split, back home to his paw. Andi, all I kin tell ya is that stranger you seen this mornin' is jest a poor feller tryin' to git hisself out of the hawg pen.

"Yes, ma'am," Andi said.

The old woman switched the conversation and didn't mention the man again. Andi followed her lead and asked no more questions. After the dishes were done, she excused herself to the trailer. She felt as tired as a plow mule on a hot, July day.

The next morning, Andi helped Sam prepare the back room to deliver Border Collie puppies. "I asked Miss Nonie about that stranger," Andi said.

"What'd she say?" Sam said.

Andi shrugged her shoulders. "Well, after telling me some long tale about a guy with a rebellious son, she said that all she could tell me is that the man I saw is just a poor fellow trying to get himself out of a hog pen."

Sam stopped sterilizing the instruments and gawked at Andi. "She said what?"

"That the stranger is just a poor man trying to get out of the hog pen," Andi repeated. "I have no clue what she was talkin' about. Do you?"

Under his breath, Sam said, "No way… it couldn't be."

"Couldn't be what?" Andi pressed.

"Nothing. Just a crazy notion. Well, I think we're ready now. Tell Katie to bring Ellie on back. Let's get this show on the road."

Katie led Ellie into the room, and Sam carefully placed her on the table. Andi petted her head and said, "You're a pretty girl. Your sweet babies will be here soon."

"Border Collies normally have large litters, and from the looks of things, she may be carrying seven or eight pups," Sam said.

As each puppy made its debut, Andi welcomed it into the world with a warm towel and then placed the little whelp in a box with a heating pad on low covered with layers of clean towels.

"One more time, girl, and I think you're done," Sam said.

When pup number seven arrived, she lay lifeless in Andi's hands. "Uh-oh, Sam," she said. "We have a problem here."

She swung the puppy back and forth, back and forth, but the teeny creature showed no signs of life. Andi rubbed her briskly with the towel. "Come on baby, breathe," she coaxed. "I'm goin' to try shockin' her system into taking a breath."

"How?" Sam said.

"Fill two pans with water, please – hot in one, but not too hot, and cold in the other," Andi said.

Sam filled the pans and placed them on the counter by the sink. Andi immersed the puppy up to her neck in the cold water and then into the hot, in the cold, then in the hot, cold, then hot. "She's wiggling!" Andi said.

Sam laughed loudly. "Well, I'll be. Would you look at that."

Andi kissed the top of the small, black head. "I think you just wanted some extra attention, Miss Priss. Come over here and meet your mama."

Andi set the newborn beside Ellie and said, "We did it!"

She raised her hand for Sam to give her five. He smiled and clapped her slender fingers with his broad palm.

"Way to go," he said.

Like Sam had warned in his first letter, the work at Bottle Knob Animal Clinic was hard, days were long, and pay was low; but Andi never complained. Determined to become a valuable asset to his veterinary practice, she quickly learned Sam's routine and labored with heart and soul from sunup to sundown. By the end of the first month, much to her relief, he hadn't mentioned releasing her.

Every evening, Nonie had supper waiting for Andi when she got home from work, and every Sunday morning, the old woman urged the girl to come with her to worship services at Bethany Primitive Baptist Church.

"Thank you, Miss Nonie," Andi said, "but not today. I think I'll just stay home and rest. It's my only day off you know."

"I know, but I promise thangs'll go a whole lot better if ya spend the first day of the week a restin' in the house of the Lord," Nonie said.

She patted Andi's hand and then climbed into the old chevy. "Honey, you jest chew on what I said fer a spell, and ya might jest come to agree I'm right."

"Yes, ma'am," Andi said.

Reflections #5

1. Andi said that she had attended church from time to time with her grandparents. Does going to church make you a Christian and get you to heaven?   YES   NO

2. How do you get to heaven? _____

3. According to the Bible, if you believe Jesus is God's Son, trust that He died in your place for your sins and rose again, and receive by faith His free gift of forgiveness and eternal life, then you are God's child and will go to heaven. Are you certain that you are a child of God and will go to heaven? YES   NO

PEARLS from God's heart to yours

_____ (your name), for by grace you have been saved through faith; and that not of yourself, it is the gift of God; not as a result of works, so that no one may boast. (Eph. 2:8-9)

_____ (your name), I go to prepare a place for you… Jesus said, "I am the way, and the truth, and the life; no one comes to the Father but through Me." (John 14:2b,6) He who has the Son has the life; he who does not have the Son of God [Jesus] does not have life. (1 John 5:12)

_____ (your name), if you confess with your mouth Jesus as Lord, and believe in your heart that God raised Him from the dead, you will be saved… for whoever will call on the name of the Lord will be saved. (Rom. 10:9,13)

PETITIONS from your heart to Jesus

_____

_____

_____

_____

_____

Chapter 6:
Watermelon Sunday

After the morning worship service, Sam saw Nonie getting in her truck and called, "Wait up, Nonie. You got a minute?"

"Hey there, doc. I got all the minutes you need. What kin I do fer ya?"

"First of all, I wanted to thank you for giving Dr. Elliott a place to stay and for bein' so kind to her," he said. "She says you're the best cook east of the Mississippi."

"Well, you best come test that tall tale out fer yerself," Nonie said. "Why don't ya join us fer Sunday dinner today? I got a pot roast in the oven, and then me and Andi figure to do a little fishin' over on Fodder Creek."

"She's goin' *fishin*'?" Sam said.

"Yep, that's what she said. Don't let her purdy, little outside fool ya, boy. That girl's got more backbone than a blue whale."

"I might just take you up on that invitation, Nonie Baskin. Thanks," Sam said. "Uh… and I also have a question. Andi said you've been helpin' a stranger back in the hollow. Who've you taken under your wing this time?"

"Aw, Sam, you know I try to help ever' poor soul the good Lord sends my way," she said and then cranked the truck. "Go on home now and git out of them Sunday duds. We'll have vittles on the table when ya git to the house."

Sam watched the old woman drive away. *Gettin' a straight answer from her really is like tryin' to squeeze blood from a turnip*, he thought.

Andi was in the kitchen setting the table when Nonie got home. "Hi, Miss Nonie," she said. "How was church?"

"Child, you missed a pow'rful good sermon," Nonie said. "Oh, and you kin set another place at the table. We're havin' company fer dinner."

"Company? Who?"

"Sam Parks," Nonie said. "And he's a goin' fishin' with us, too."

Her face brightened. "You're kiddin'. Now that's a surprise."

Andi sang softly as she pulled another plate from the cupboard and placed a carefully folded napkin under each fork.

"You've got a purdy voice. Is that 'You are My Sunshine' yo're a singin'?" Nonie said.

"Yes, ma'am, one of my grandmother's favorites. I remember her singin' that and rockin' me when I was a little girl."

Nonie looked out the kitchen window, but her gaze seemed to fall past the mountains onto times gone by. "That's a precious memory, Andi. Don't ever let it slip out of yer heart. Ya hear?"

Andi hugged her friend. "I won't," she said. "You're a special lady, Miss Nonie. I love you."

An hour later, Sam carried his plate to the sink. "Thank you for that delicious meal," he said. "Andi's right. You are the best cook east of the Mississippi – next to my mom that is."

"Why thank ya kindly," Nonie said. "Now, we have some fishin' to do. Sam, take this here tin can and Mason jar. Thar's a worm box behind the shed where you'll find the night crawlers and a tree beside the barn with catalpa worms. Bring Andi with ya, and git the fishin' poles out of the shed while yer at it. Y'all load ever'thang in my truck, and I'll be out in a jiffy after I tidy up a bit."

Andi strolled with Sam to the old toolshed. A gentle breeze across the hollow cooled the blaring August sun hanging in a sky as blue as the cornflowers in Nonie's vegetable garden. Honeybees buzzed from blossom to blossom, and cicadas crooned their most spirited song in the warm, summer air.

She lifted the lid of the wooden box sitting on a rickety table, and her hazel eyes glowed like lanterns. "Oh, Sam," she said. "This worm bed's just like my granddaddy's."

Using a small gardening trowel, she shoveled rich, brown dirt laden with wiggly worms into the tin can. Sam stuffed large leaves crawling with green and black striped catalpa worms into the jar, punched holes in the top with his pocketknife, and then grabbed three cane poles from the shed.

Nonie joined them at the truck and handed Sam the keys. "You drive," she said. But instead of getting in the vehicle, she started toward the garden.

"Where you goin'?" Sam called.

"To pick our watermelon, of course. It ain't a summer Sunday without a juicy-sweet, red-ripe melon."

Fodder Creek ran a zigzag race down Laurel Mountain, and then leaped into the Hiwassee River just a few miles east of Nonie's farm. Sam parked on the roadside, and the old woman led her young companions up a gnarled path where they heard the rushing rivulet a good piece before they spied it.

"On the first shelf of the mountain," Nonie said, "the creek calms to a wide pool fer sum mighty fine fishin'. Sam, I 'member yer grandpaw a bringin' you and yer brother up here when you wuz young'uns."

"Yes, ma'am, he did," Sam said.

30

"Andi, you ever heared 'bout the feller who got et by a fish?" Nonie said.

"You mean Jonah? Now that's one Bible story I have heard," Andi said.

There was no stopping the old storyteller, however, from spouting her rendition of the holy fish tale. "Well, one day, the Lord called down from whar the thunder hides to a feller named Jonah and said, 'Jonah! Hey, Jonah! Git up and scoot on down to Ninevah and preach to them wicked folks.' Jonah got up all right, but 'stead of scurryin' off to Nivevah, he slipped down to Joppa and boarded a ship headed for Tarshish. The Lord warn't fooled one ounce though. He knew 'xactly whar ol' Jonah wuz a hidin'. So God hurled a great wind on the sea so ferocious that the ship wuz jest about to be tore to pieces. Jonah knowed the gale wuz his fault fer a disobeyin' God; so he said, 'Throw me overboard, boys, and this here storm'll stop.'"

Sam bit his lip to keep a straight face and cast his line farther up the creek.

"As soon as Jonah hit them high waves," Nonie said, "the Lord appointed a great fish to swaller him up. All that poor man could do wuz jest set thar in the critter's belly and pray fer three dark days and three dark nights. But in the stink of his situation, Jonah changed his wayward tune in a Tennessee minute from no-way-Hosea to yes-Sirree-whatever-You-need!"

Unable to contain himself any longer, Sam howled with laughter.

"It's true, doc. Jest look it up in the Scriptures fer yerself." Nonie said.

Sam grinned like a Cheshire cat. "Yes, ma'am, I know it's true. I've probably heard that story a thousand times; but I gotta admit your version wins first prize, hands down."

"Well, anyways, the Lord had it planned out all along to give ole Jonah a second chance. So God commanded the fish to spit that scallywag out on dry land — splat! Jonah staggered to his feet, wiped the whale slobber from his chin, and off he went to Ninevah. Andi, Jonah wuz fer real that giant fish wuz fer real, and God's real too – jest as real as that shagbark hickory yo're a leanin' against. He's always a chasin' after good folks, as well as the ornery ones, with His goodness and His mercy, and He's closer than the very air we breathe. A body's jest a wastin' time tryin' to run or hide from Almighty God. Ain't that right, Sam."

"That's right. Jesus knows right where we are all the time - just like He knows where all the fish in Fodder Creek are hidin' this afternoon."

Just then, Andi's bobber disappeared under the water. "I got one!" she shouted and pulled a lively rainbow trout from the mountain stream. Nonie looked up and winked toward heaven.

Reflections #6

POINTS to Ponder

1. What story did Nonie tell Andi and Sam? The story of _____. In this true Bible story, Jonah got on a ship in an attempt to _____ away from God.

2. Nonie said that God is _____ than the air we breathe; therefore, no one can _____ from God.

3. Have you ever run away from God or tried to hide from Him?   YES   NO

   If so, why did you leave? _____

   _____

PEARLS from God's heart to yours

_____ (your name), I search you and know you. I know when you sit down and when you rise up; I understand your thoughts from afar... Where can you go from My Spirit? Or where can you flee from My Presence? (Psalm 139:1-2,7)

_____ (your name), I am your Shepherd... fear no evil, for I am with you... surely My goodness and lovingkindness will follow you all the days of your life. (Psalm 23:1,4,6)

_____ (your name), O taste and see that I am good; how blessed is the one who takes refuge in Me... My eyes are toward you, and My ears are open to your cry... I am near to the brokenhearted, and I save those who are crushed in spirit. (Psalm 34:8,15,18)

PETITIONS from your heart to Jesus

_____

_____

_____

_____

Chapter 7:
A Little Talk With Jesus

Long, afternoon shadows covered Hoot Owl Hollow by the time the threesome returned to Nonie's farm. "Ladies," Sam said, "thank you for the tasty lunch and charming company. I thoroughly enjoyed both."

"Come back anytime, Sam," Nonie said.

Andi said, "See you in the mornin'."

On his way out of the cove, Sam saw a pair of mallards glide in and out of the thick cattails in Nonie's pond. Across the road, a squirrel chattered loudly at the blue jay competing for his river birch limb; but it was a movement deeper in the woods that captured Sam's attention. *Was that somebody?* he thought.

He stopped the truck and walked to the rail fence. "Hello! Anybody there?"

No one answered, but a startled rabbit hopped into the thicket. "Now, I'm seeing ghosts," he said and climbed back in his truck.

After the taillights disappeared over the hill, a tall man stepped from behind a large oak tree and hiked the narrow trail up Raccoon Mountain.

The bright skies soon faded to an ebony canvas splattered with twinkling stars. On Sam's back porch, the young man rocked back and forth, back and forth clutching an old, leather Bible. His great, great grandfather – the Rev. Harold S. Parks, an Appalachian Mountain circuit rider – originally owned this prized, family heirloom. The chocolate Lab sleeping at Sam's feet, sat up when the who-who-ha-who, who-who-ha-who of a hoot owl drifted through the darkness. He scratched behind the dog's ears and said, "It's okay, Joe."

Sam studied the Big Dipper and Little Dipper hanging in the heavens. "Lord," he said, "You certainly stumped me this time. I asked for a pair of strong hands to help at the clinic, and in walks Andi. She may not have muscles, but she sure is a good vet. Still Your word says as plain as day, 'Do not be unequally yoked together with unbelievers,' and she's not a Christian. So what am I supposed to do? I don't really understand what You're up to."

No sooner had Sam voiced his concerns than he remembered the Scripture: faith comes from hearing and hearing by the word of Christ. He turned the tattered pages of the timeworn Bible to Romans chapter 10 and read, "How will they call on Him in whom they have not believed? How will they believe in Him whom they have not heard? And how will they hear without a preacher? How will they preach unless they are sent? Just as it is written, 'How beautiful are the feet of those who bring good news of good things.' So faith comes from hearing, and hearing by the word of Christ."

He nodded thoughtfully. "So — maybe this isn't about the clinic and me after all. Maybe it's about what You're up to in *Andi's* life. Well, if faith comes by hearing Your word, then what better place to plant an unbeliever than right in the middle of Hoot Owl Hollow at Nonie Baskin's kitchen table. Father, please help Andi understand Your plan for salvation. Please give her faith to believe in Your Son, Jesus; and Lord, please show me my part in Your plans."

Sam sat quietly and watched the silver moon climb over the treetops. Verses from Isaiah 43, hidden in his heart since childhood, scrolled across his mind, "You are My witnesses," declares the Lord, "And My servants whom I have chosen, so that you may know and believe Me and understand that I am He, the Lord, and there is no savior besides Me. Behold, I will do something new. I will even make a roadway in the wilderness, rivers in the desert."

Sam said, "I'll be a witness, Lord; but You, and only You, can convert her thirsty soul into a well-watered garden. Thank You for what You're doing and for the new things yet to come. In Jesus' name I pray, amen."

The heat of summertime slowly surrendered to cooler, colorful autumn days. Fiery sunrises set ablaze the crimson and gold mantle shrouding the North Georgia Mountains, and velvet, bejeweled nights trailed early sunsets.

"What's on our schedule today?" Andi asked Sam when she got to the clinic one chilly, October morning.

"Do you mind working here while I go on calls?" Sam said. "Oscar Wheeler's cow has a breech calf, Dan Walker's mare somehow got out of the fence and stepped in a huntin' trap, and then on top of that, Mrs. Edge wants me to check her mule. She's afraid he's goin' lame."

"Sounds like you've got a full day ahead of you," Andi said. "Of course I don't mind. Go on, Sam. I'll be fine."

He climbed in the truck and said, "Just call on the radio if you have any trouble."

"I will. And don't hesitate to call me if you need help," she teased.

"Okay, will do," he said and grinned. Leaving the clinic, he glanced at Andi in the rearview mirror. *Lord, You know I really like Andi; but according to the Bible, since I'm a Christian, I shouldn't even consider courting her till she's Yours. Please save that lady soon, Lord Jesus - for her sake and mine.*

Before she could unlock the front door, a Ford Bronco, older than Andi herself, pulled into the parking lot. Mr. Brown from the post office got out holding his longhaired Siamese, Gracie, in a wire carrier.

"Hey, Mr. Brown," Andi said. "Come on in. I'm just opening up. Sam's out in the county today, but I'll be happy to take a look at Gracie, if that's okay with you."

Fred Brown gave her a fatherly hug. "That's just fine with me and Gracie, too," he said. "You've proved to be a mighty fine vet, Miss Andi. But I gotta tell ya' I wuz a tad skeptical the first day you come to the post office askin' fer directions."

During Gracie's examination, Sarah Archibald arrived with her beloved pug, Maxine, and a steady stream of patrons and their animals flowed right behind. *Whew!* Andi thought, *it's harder than I imagined without Sam here.*

At the end of the busy day, the young woman crawled into her beetle to go home, but when she turned the key nothing happened. She pumped the accelerator and tried again to no avail. Thankfully, however, Sam pulled up beside her.

He rolled down his window and said, "Havin' trouble?"

"Boy, am I glad to see you," Andi said. "I think my battery's dead."

"Hop out and let me try," he said.

After several more unsuccessful attempts and a fast check under the hood, Sam said, "Yep, I think your right – the battery's as dead as a doornail. I loaned my jumper cables to Jim Shoemaker last week, so we'll have to wait till tomorrow to get it started. Just leave your car here tonight. I'll take you home and pick you back up in the mornin'."

"Okay, thanks," she said.

Sam accompanied her to the passenger side of his truck and opened the door. Although the initial tension between Sam and Andi had relaxed to a pleasant friendship, he'd never before shown her this kind of courtesy. She gave him a questioning look and repeated, "Thank you, Sam."

Near the turn to Nonie's farm, Andi said, "Take the next right."

"Yeah, I know," Sam said. "I grew up in Bottle Knob. Remember?"

"Of course. I'm so worn out I'm not thinkin' straight," she said. "I don't see how you ran the clinic all by yourself."

When they came around the first bend of Hoot Owl Hollow, a man, standing in the road, froze in the headlights. Andi said, "Watch out!"

Sam hit the brakes, and both doctors jumped from the truck and ran after the hollow "phantom" fleeing into the trees. "Wait!" Sam yelled. "Please! Come back."

In the shadowy woods, Andi said, "That's the stranger I've been telling you about."

Sam stared into the darkness. "That's no stranger, Andi. He's my brother."

Reflections #7

POINTS to Ponder

1. When Sam prayed, he talked to God as a friend. Can someone really become a friend of God?   YES   NO   (Read John 15:14-15 and James 2:23)

2. How did God "talk" to Sam and answer his questions? _____

   _____

3. Sam made decisions according to God's word rather than his own wants. Are

   your choices determined by your desires or God's commands? _____

   _____

PEARLS from God's heart to yours

_____ (your name), there is a friend who sticks closer than a brother [His name is Jesus]. (Prov. 18:24)

_____ (your name), all Scripture is inspired by Me and profitable for teaching, for reproof, for correction, for training in righteousness; so that My people may be adequate, equipped for every good work. (2 Tim. 3:16-17)

_____ (your name), My word is a lamp to your feet and a light to your path. (Psalm 119:105)

PETITIONS from your heart to Jesus

_____

_____

_____

_____

_____

Chapter 8:
Paul

Andi gasped. "Your brother! What do you mean he's your brother?"

Sam looked down at Andi. "Just what I said. That man's my older brother, Paul. I haven't seen him in fifteen years. He ran away when he was seventeen and I was fourteen. Come on," Sam said, pulling Andi by the arm. "I need to talk to Nonie."

Sam and Andi charged through Nonie's front door without even knocking and found her frying fish in the kitchen.

"Well, howdy Sam," Nonie said. "Glad you could join us fer supper. Andi, set another place at the table, please."

"Paul's the stranger in the woods, isn't he? And you've been helping him, haven't you." Sam said. "What on earth is going on? And why didn't you tell me?"

"You kids go wash yer hands now, and we'll talk over catfish and hushpuppies," Nonie said. "Go on now — git!"

There was no arguing with Nonie Baskin or hurrying her to give a quick answer. So Sam and Andi obediently cleaned up for supper and sat down with Nonie around the pine board table.

Nonie reached for Sam and Andi's hands and prayed, "Lord Jesus, thank Ye fer another good day. Thank Ye fer this food we're about to eat, and thank Ye that we kin be a trustin' in You more than the thangs we see or feel. Amen."

"Miss Nonie, Paul's been missing for *fifteen* years. Please, you've gotta tell me everything you know," Sam said.

Nonie turned to Andi. "Andi, you ever heared of a feller named Saul?"

Oh no. Here she goes again, Andi thought and then said, "No, ma'am, but Miss Nonie, I don't think this is a good time to —"

"It's okay," Sam interrupted. "Let her speak her mind."

"Thank ya, Sam," Nonie said with satisfaction. "Well, ya see, in the New Testamint, thar wuz this feller named Saul. He figured hisself to be powerful religious, he did; but that Saul, he hated Christians. So he commenced to breathin' threats down thar necks and a throwin' 'em into jail. One day, Saul wuz on his way down to a town called Damascus to git all them people belongin' to The Way — that's what they called the church folks back then — when all of a sudden, a light come flashin' down from heaven so bright that it knocked ole Saul plumb to the ground. And a voice boomed, 'Saul, Saul, what's the matter with you? Why are you a persecutin Me?' Saul cried back, 'Who are ya, Lord?' And the voice thundered, "I'm Jesus. Now git up and git yerself on into town, and I'll be a tellin' ya what to do."

Sam listened patiently.

"Well, when Saul got up, he wuz as blind as a bat; so some other fellers had to come and lead him by the hand like a little child on into town. Ole Saul jest sat thar prayin' fer three black days — not able to see nothing; till finally, Jesus sent a man named Ananias to visit him. When Ananias got thar, he put his hands on Saul. And low and behold, the Holy Ghost come all over that man like a chicken on a June bug and filled him up to the brim. Then somethin' like scales done fell off of his eyes. Saul wuz healed! He could see. He commenced to a praisin' Jesus like nobody's business and tellin' ever'body that Jesus truly is the Son of God."

Nonie turned back to Sam and said, "Sam, your brother Paul's done seen the light. He knows what he done to the church wuz wrong, and Jesus has saved him from his sins; but he jest cain't forgive hisself. That ole devil's got him convinced that he's the scum of earth fer a settin' the church on fire."

"He burned the chu—" Andi started, but caught herself and hushed.

"He thanks ever'body hates him, and nobody kin ever forgive him," Nonie said. "So, I've jest been a doctorin' his wounded heart with a little healin' salve of Christian love. I wuz aimin' to tell you when the time wuz right. Truly, I wuz."

"When did he come back?" Sam said. "Where's he stayin'?"

"Oh, let me thank. I believe the first time I seen him wuz pert near a year ago. I caught a glimpse of somebody in the woods, and I suspicioned it might be Paul. I figured he might be a hidin' out in that old huntin' shack my grandpaw built up on Raccoon Mountain, so I started leavin' some food and supplies up thar from time to time. After a few weeks, he trusted me to be a friend, and we been visitin' regular ever' since," Nonie said.

Sam stood up. "I'm goin' up to that cabin right now."

Nonie drew him back toward the chair. "Set yerself back down here. You gotta wait on the Lord and let Him set the pace. Patience always brings good fruit. I'll talk to Paul and see if he's ready to face you; but first, tell me what's in yer heart."

"I've been prayin' for Paul for years — my whole family has been. We love him, and we all forgave him a long ti…." Sam's voice broke and tears filled his blue eyes.

The old woman patted Sam's hand. "Don't you be a fearin' now. The Lord said in the book of Jeremiah, 'I will give 'em a heart to know Me, for I am the Lord; and they'll be My people, and I'll be their God, for they will return to Me with their whole heart.' The Lord's a bringin' Paul back — back to Hisself first, and then He'll bring him back to yer family. You jest gotta trust Him to do it His way and in His time."

"Yes, ma'am," Sam said and then leaned over and kissed his wise friend. "Thank you, Miss Nonie, for helpin' my brother."

After Sam left, Andi dried the dishes Nonie washed and asked, "Can you tell me more about what happened with Paul?"

"I reckin I kin since you know most of the story now anyways," Nonie said. "Well, ya know Sam and Paul's daddy is our preacher down at Bethany."

"No, I didn't know that," Andi said.

"Thar's lots of thangs you don't know, girl, 'cause you been missin' the possibilities the Lord's been puttin' right in front of yer purdy face," Nonie said gently. "Anyhow, Paul's jest like his paw in lots of ways and that made fer sum fearsome head buttin' between Pastor Parks and his oldest boy. Well, somethin' happened one night between 'em, — some sort of silly argument that got Paul all riled up - madder than a wet hen in a rainstorm. And bein' a reckless youngun', he lashed out at his paw by runnin' out and settin' the church on fire. A neighbor seen the flames and put it out before the church burned down, but I reckin Paul wuz so ashamed of hisself and what he done that he jest took off. Nobody seen hide nor hair of that boy till a year or so ago when I seen him in the woods of Hoot Owl Holler. His family never give up on him, though. His maw and paw pray ever'day — askin' the Lord to bring thar boy home."

Andi rubbed the drying cloth around and around and around the cast iron skillet and then set it in the warm oven to finish drying. "Miss Nonie," Andi said. "I think I'd like to go to church with you next Sunday. Is that okay?"

"Of course it is, child," Nonie said. She dropped the wet dishrag and hugged the girl. "Course it is!"

On Sunday, Nonie guided the old Chevy down a gravel road and parked beside the Primitive Baptist Church. A traditional steeple holding a cross topped the white-frame, one-room sanctuary nestled beneath towering oaks and hickory trees. Andi saw a tall man with grey hair ringing the church bell and welcoming the parishioners. *Oh my goodness, that has to be Sam's dad,* she thought. *He looks just like him.*

"Preacher, I'd like fer ye to meet Andi Elliott. She works with yer boy, Sam, and lives in my trailer in Hoot Owl Holler," Nonie said.

Pastor Parks shook Andi's hand in both of his and said, "What a pleasure to meet you, Dr. Elliott. I've heard so many wonderful things about you. Thank you for comin' today. God bless you."

Nonie introduced Andi to every person between the front door and the third pew from the pulpit – her regular seat for more than sixty years. Andi looked across the aisle and caught Sam watching her and smiling. She smiled back and waved.

After a rousing chorus of "Savior, Like a Shepherd Lead Us", "Blessed Be the Name", and "Love Lifted Me", Pastor Parks stepped to the platform.

"Good morning," he said cheerfully.

"Good morning, pastor," the congregation responded.

"This is the day which the Lord hath made," he said.

"We will rejoice and be glad in it," they answered.

"Open your Bibles, please, to Ephesians chapter 3 verses 14 through 21 and follow along as I read from the King James translation. 'For this cause I bow my knees unto the Father of our Lord Jesus Christ, of whom the whole family in heaven and earth is named, that He would grant you, according to the riches of His glory, to be strengthened with might by His Spirit in the inner man; that Christ may dwell in your hearts by faith; that ye, being rooted and grounded in love, may be able to comprehend with all saints what is the breadth, and length, and depth, and height; and to know the love of Christ, which passeth knowledge, that ye might be filled with all the fullness of God. Now unto Him that is able to do exceeding abundantly above all that we ask or think, according to the power that worketh in us, unto Him be the glory in the church by Christ Je— '"

At that moment, the door creaked in the rear of the small auditorium, and Pastor Parks stopped midsentence. Andi, along with the entire assembly, turned to see what had paralyzed the minister. There stood Paul.

Reflections #8

POINTS to Ponder

1. What sin had Paul committed as a teenager? _____

   _____

   Even though Jesus had forgiven his sin, Paul could not _____ himself.

2. Is it difficult for you to forgive yourself for your sins?   YES   NO

3. Read 1 John 1:9 and fill in the blanks: "If we _____ our sins, [God] is

   faithful and righteous to _____ us our sins and to _____ us from all righteousness."

PEARLS from God's heart to yours

_____ (your name), though your sins are as scarlet, they will be as white as snow; though they are red like crimson, they will be as wool. (Isaiah 1:18)

_____ (your name), as far as the east is from the west, so far have I removed your transgressions (sins) from you. (Psalm 103:12)

_____ (your name), in Him (Jesus) you have redemption through His blood, the forgiveness of your trespasses (sins), according to the riches of His grace. (Eph. 1:7)

PETITIONS from your heart to Jesus

_____

_____

_____

_____

_____

Chapter 9:
Lost and Found

P astor Parks dropped the heavy Bible on the podium and ran with outstretched arms toward his firstborn. Sam jumped to his feet and followed his dad. Mrs. Parks cried, "Thank You, Lord Jesus! Thank You!" and made her way between the pews to join her family huddled in the center aisle.

The congregation joined Nonie as she warbled, "Amazing Grace how sweet the sound, that saved a wretch like me. I once was lost, but now am found, was blind, but now I see."

Tears spilled from Andi's eyes. She closed them tightly and prayed, *Oh God, I want to know You, too. Please help me.*

The pastor's voice could be heard above the crowd. "Praise God!" he said. "Glory, Hallelujah! My boy was lost but now he's found. Praise God!!"

The people shouted, "Amen! Praise the Lord!"

After several minutes of celebration, the room fell still when Pastor Parks walked back to the pulpit.

"Beloved, there may be others here today who are lost – separated from Holy God by your unforgiven sin.

Brothers and sisters, I declare to you the gospel from 1 Corinthians chapter 15, that Christ died for your sins according to the Scriptures; and that He was buried, and that He rose again the third day. Romans 10:9 says that if thou shalt confess with thy mouth the Lord Jesus, and shalt believe in thine heart that God hath raised Him from the dead, thou shalt be saved! Delay it no longer, my children. Today is the day of salvation. Be converted; be born again. You who are lost may be found. Who will come? Who will come to Father God for salvation through faith in His Son, Jesus Christ?"

In a rich, baritone voice, the pastor led his flock in singing, "Just as I am, without one plea, but that Thy blood was shed for me, and that Thou bidd'st me come to Thee, O Lamb of God, I come, I come."

On the second stanza, Andi left her seat and approached the pastor now standing in front of the altar. "I want to know, Jesus," Andi said. "I want to ask God for forgiveness of my sins and His free gift of eternal life."

Pastor Parks prayed with Andi while the people of Bethany Baptist sang, "Just as I am, Thou wilt receive, wilt welcome, pardon, cleanse, relieve, because Thy promise I believe, O Lamb of God, I come! I come!"

The following week, Bottle Knob was all abuzz with the good news of their prodigal son's return, as well as, the salvation of their lady veterinarian. Those two miracles sparked a fresh joy in the community that ignited random acts of kindness and loving-neighbors-as-themselves.

On Tuesday afternoon, Andi filled her car with gas and then went inside the local station to pay; but Mr. Adams just smiled and said, "No, ma'am. This tank's on me."

Sam urged his brother to live with him and help at the clinic till he could get on his feet. Paul accepted his invitation with humble gratitude and worked eagerly — doing any and everything Sam asked. Having another pair of strong hands around proved valuable to both Sam and Andi.

Toward the end of the week, Sam helped Paul mend the back, screen door and thought, *Well, Lord, You did it. You brought Paul home, You saved Andi, and in Your own time and way, You provided even more help than I asked for. Thank You, Lord Jesus.*

"Ben Eller called," Sam said. "Do you remember him? I think he was a grade or two ahead of you in school. Anyway, he owns a farm out in Wills Valley and wants Andi and me to come check his cattle. He's experimenting with a new calving program this fall. Wanna come with us?"

Andi looked like a little child sandwiched in-between the strapping Parks brothers on the bench seat of Sam's truck. She enjoyed listening to their ragging.

In her mind, she prayed, *You are amazing, Lord. Miss Nonie says You promised in the book of Joel to restore the years that the locusts have eaten. Sam and Paul have picked up right where they left off - just as though no time was lost at all. What a wonderful God You are. Thank You for rescuing Paul and me.*

Sam, Andi, and Paul piled out of the truck, and Ben Eller hurried toward them in long, quick strides. "Welcome home, Paul!" Ben said, shaking his hand and hugging him at the same time. "It's good to see you, man. It's so good to see you."

Andi felt like a fifth wheel as the three men talked over old times and remember-whens, so she quietly slipped away and walked past the barn to Ben's pasture. Twin calves stood about ten feet from the fence and peered at the girl through large, curious eyes. Both babies had matching white faces, soft brown ears, and solid brown bodies except for heart-shaped, white spots on their little chests.

She slowly opened the gate so as not to startle them and eased toward the calves. "Hey babies. You have beautiful markings. Where's your mama?" Andi said.

Meanwhile, Sam looked around and noticed Andi was missing. "Where's Andi?" he said.

"That girl loves critters," Paul said. "She probably went to see the calves."

"I hope she didn't go inside the fence," Ben said. "I've got one cow that charges anybody that comes within twenty feet of her babies."

"Oh, no," Sam said and then took off like a sprinter in a fifty-yard dash.

"Andi!" he yelled. "Andi! Where are you?"

As he rounded the corner of the barn, Sam saw a cow, with horned-head lowered, storming straight toward Andi. "Look out, Andi! Behind you!"

Petrified by fear, the girl couldn't move. Sam raced through the gate, grabbed Andi's forearm, and jerked her back with such force that she landed on the ground several feet behind him. He slammed the gate closed just as the angry mama butted the fence.

He knelt down beside his pale colleague and said, "Are you okay, Andi? Are you hurt?"

She saw the concern on Sam's face and tried to hold back hot tears. "Yeah, I'm fine. Really, I'm fine. I'm sorry, Sam. I am so sorry."

"You could've been killed, you know."

"I know. I'm so sorry," she repeated softly.

The other two men rushed to where the pair was sitting. Paul gave Sam a hand up, and Ben helped Andi. "Ma'am, I apologize. I should've warned you about Gertie. She's like a wild bear defending her cubs. I was so excited to see Paul that I just wasn't thinkin'," Ben said.

"That makes two of us," Andi said. "Thank you all. Sorry for the scare."

Paul tried to ease Andi's embarrassment. "Well, thank Goodness everybody's okay," he said. "Uh, Ben, why don't you show us that new calvin' program you've been bragging so much about."

No one spoke a word on the long ride back. When they got to the clinic, Paul said, "I better go clean the kennels," and then disappeared behind the building. Sam and Andi marched inside and passed Katie's desk without acknowledging her.

"What's the matter with you two?" Katie said. "You look as gloomy as a graveyard on a wet Sunday."

Sam didn't answer, but Andi said, "Oh, hi Katie. We're okay. I just messed up royally today. That's all."

She followed Sam into the back room and closed the door.

"Sam, on the first day I came, I gave you my word that I'd leave if I ever came close to getting' hurt. A promise is a promise; so I guess I'm done. I'll finish out this week if that's okay with you and go on back to Atlanta on Saturday. I want to thank you for letting me work at Bottle Knob. I'm so sorry things didn't work out. I really love it up here, and I'll never forget yo…. I'll never forget all the wonderful people in this town," she said.

Sam walked over to Andi, lifted her face in his hands, and with his thumbs, tenderly wiped the tears from her cheeks. "Andi," he said. "I'd like for you to stay. I want you to stay, and I promise I'll do a better job taking care of you if you do. And I need to ask you a question. I know you gave your heart to Jesus last Sunday, but is there enough room in there for me, too?"

Andi stood on her tiptoes and kissed Sam's cheek. "Yes!" she said and then threw both arms around his burly neck.

Sam returned the hug and silently prayed, *Thank You, Lord Jesus. You have done far more abundantly beyond my wildest dreams. To You be all the glory down through every generation forever and ever. Amen.*

Author's Reflections

Dear Reader,

Thank you for reading *Hoot Owl Hollow*. While tracking Andi's adventures through the North Georgia Mountains, I hope you've considered your own relationship with God. Every person on this ol' earth is God's creation; but according to John 1:12, only those who believe in the name of God's Son, Jesus, and receive Him are given the right to become God's children. Are you a child of God?

Have you ever heard of a fellow named Nicodemus? Well, one night long ago, a Pharisee called Nicodemus came secretly to Jesus. Jesus said, "Truly, truly, I say to you, unless you are born again you cannot see the kingdom of God." (In other words, you'll never see heaven.) Amazed, Nicodemus said, "How can someone be born again?" Jesus explained that everyone is born physically, but to be born again you must be reborn spiritually by believing in Him. *"For God so loved the world that He gave His only begotten Son, Jesus, that whoever believes in Him shall not perish but have eternal life" (John 3:16), and "as many as receive Jesus, to them He gives the right to become children of God, even to those who believe in His name, who are born, not of blood nor... of the will of man, but of God" (John 1:12-13).*

You do the believing; God does the rebirthing. He forgives, removes sins, and gives you forever after, never-ending life with Him. It's a free gift that isn't deserved and can't be earned; but by believing and trusting Jesus, you can have it! Like Andi in this story, if you want to receive God's free gift of everlasting life, then ask Him right now - ask to be born again. If you just did that, then welcome to the family, O child of God.

Jill Watson Glassco

Afterword

As a teenager, instead of counting sheep, I sometimes told myself stories to get to sleep. Andi's adventure in the mountains of North Georgia is one of my long-ago, bedtime sedatives.

Along the pages of *Hoot Owl Hollow* in the character of the wise and lion-hearted Nonie Baskin are footprints of six extraordinary women: Verna Watson (my mother), Imogene Glassco (my mother-in-law), Willie Elliott, Alandra Parks, Evelyn Baskin, and Nonie Webb. These "steel magnolias" blazed a live-life-righteously-and-courageously trail I aspire to follow.

Although the story and characters of *Hoot Owl Hollow* are fictitious, our friend Elizabeth Edge lives in the real Hoot Owl Hollow tucked beneath the North Georgia Mountains near the town of Hiwassee. Years ago, when I first visited her with my husband's family, they told me not to cut my foot as I walked to the trailer sitting in Liz's cow pasture. To this day, I'm still teased about looking for "broken glass".

Jill